Music
from Home

Selected Poems

by

Colleen J. McElroy

With Preface by John Gardner
And an Introduction by Knute Skinner

Southern Illinois University Press
Carbondale and Edwardsville

Feffer & Simons, Inc.
London and Amsterdam

Library of Congress Cataloging in Publication Data
McElroy, Colleen J.
   Music from home.
    I. Title.
PS3563.A2925A6   1976   811'.5'4   76–14852
ISBN 0–8093–0774–X

For David

Contents

Preface

By John Gardner

It is frequently said—and it's true, I think—that there are more good poets writing in America at the present time than ever before, so many that some of them, even some of the best, never get a proper hearing. There are readers enough—far more readers, I'm convinced, than most publishers imagine—and by readers I mean not only people who skim through the poetry books in their town or college libraries, but also people who actually buy books of poetry. And there are magazines enough, from the *New Yorker* and the *American Poetry Review* to those queerly named magazines that surface for an issue or two and then vanish, to be replaced by some other queer name. But there are not enough dedicated publishers of books of poetry. Though poetry books do sell, to some extent, they don't sell in the kind of volume commercial publishing generally insists on. All the best series have long waiting lists, so that even poets of acknowledged stature must chew at their nails for years before their books see print.

I'd thought for some time of trying to get a new series started at the Southern Illinois University Press, if I could just find an experienced editor of poetry who'd be willing to help me with it—for no money. At university presses that's the usual arrangement: you believe in a thing and get the press to help you do it. If the book breaks even, or the Government gives you a grant to cover your losses, the General Editor buys you a martini. Which is enough, in fact. The freedom to do what you believe in is usually more expensive. After five years of hunting for exactly the right editor, I ran into Knute Skinner, with whom I'd worked long before on the *Western Review*. He gulped once or twice at the enormity of the thing I was asking of him—collecting, sifting, and editing manuscripts can be full-time work. But he agreed to help me. We decided together that the usual slim, handsome volume of poems would not satisfy us. There was too much good poetry waiting to be printed—poetry like that of Colleen McElroy, a poet extremely good, I think you'll find. We decided (to put it bluntly) on fat, cheap books—not elegant little volumes but thick selections of the best poems by neglected poets. As a general rule we plan, if all goes well, to print neglected American poets; occasionally we may print a neglected English-speaking poet from, say, Ireland. Whatever glory there may be in the project we've agreed to share equally. Such is the history of the Sagittarius Poetry Series. Colleen McElroy's poetry should be sufficient proof that such a series is needed.

I hardly know where to begin my praise of Colleen McElroy's poetry. One might start with the authority and purity of the voice, not a well-constructed artifice of the kind one encounters too often in contemporary poetry, but a singing instrument, flexible, capable of gentleness, humor, sorrow, unwhining pain, above all, love; a voice forgiving and wise as an old woman's, sometimes shy and teasing, like the voice of a young girl, sometimes sharp for a moment, full of anger, sometimes outrageous and funny and black-earthy; and always, whatever the mood, a voice full of goodness—a rare commodity—full of Colleen McElroy's deep-down love of what is good, what is flavorful, what is just. Or one might start with the emotional precision of her images:

> Papa's not too hard to understand;
>   he was just a man
> With a hawkish face and long steps
> Ending in feet that emptied puddles.

Or:

> The sidewalks were long where I grew up,
> They were as veined as the backs
> Of my Grandma's hands.

Or one might start with the fact that she's absolutely, self-confidently a woman:

> The cat pacing the house at night
> daintily steps over what we were.
> While your nostrils flare
> into the wind sniffing spring thaw,
> your hands lock on my hips
> claiming the woman you say I am.

Or the fact that she's also wonderfully, brazenly, black:

> White folks always sitting around
> comparing their knots
> my left ball is Czechoslovakian
> my right one is Hungarian . . .

It's that joyful assertion of what she is that makes her poetry universal.

Carbondale, Illinois
September 1975

Introduction

By Knute Skinner

The publication of *Music from Home* will bring Colleen McElroy additional readers, but obviously her poetry must be good if she is to hold an audience. Her poetry must reflect her time (the Age of McElroy), and it must reveal her as an interesting person. It must speak with wisdom as well as emotion, and it must give us something we need to know or be reminded of. It must have memorable language and detail.

From first to last, McElroy's poetry performs these wonders. In Part I of *Music from Home* there is a group of poems describing the poet's childhood and its associations. McElroy sometimes calls these her anecdotal poems, but they are never merely anecdotal. From them emerges a world of people worth knowing about. There is a playmate, Pussy, who "ain't got no abacus" but who is the best at jumping Double-Dutch. There's Old Man Farrow, who sells "hog-mogonized" milk in his dirty store. There's George Darlington Love, a first beau. There's Pussy's uncle, Crazy Max, who hung onto the porch railing "like a rag doll" before falling to his death. There are the neighborhood school children buying pickles and peppermint at the Jew's.

Most importantly there are the relatives. Mama's sisters have oak legs, and the biggest of them, Claudia, "takes cabs to prove she's city." Brother is "never mentioned without / His hooked nose." Uncle Roman's son had five reasons for dying. Gra'ma spent her youth "scrubbing, serving and suckling / Pink babies." Daddy's "nostrils expand / Like black pearls." He believes in his army career but his "memories aren't the right color / For the local VFW."

Papa, McElroy's grandfather, "stands high watching white folks / Slide by the brewery stable where / He kept the horses fine." He seems to me a real person, as alive now as he was when he paced in front of a fourposter and counted eight times before getting a son. Or when he "sat high in his '29 Ford/With Uncle Lewis' wife in a summer hat." If someone were to offer me proof that Papa never existed, I couldn't accept it, for I have seen the real evidence in these poems.

McElroy's people do not live exemplary lives (perhaps), but they emerge with fine qualities of strength and endurance. They are portrayed with a combination of affection and insight and—above all—humor. McElroy's humor, with which she describes herself as well as others, is a versatile instrument. It can make us smile or laugh but, more importantly, it embodies the perspective from which her mind, mature and understanding, recreates experience.

From the first line of the book, where we find her sitting "crotch-high" under a table of relatives, McElroy's sense of humor is evident. It does more than adorn the poems, and it is absolutely necessary to their existence. Take for example this passage from "The End of Sisterhood":

> The smell of sandlot dirt and sound of
>   blue jean zippers
> Ends one final groping, ends sisterhood.
> Nothing ventured, nothing gained.
> So I bang into full bloom
> Stunned by pain.

Here the author sees experience with double eyesight, from the viewpoint of the participant and simultaneously from that of the adult looking back. A superimposed view is conveyed through time, as Roethke conveyed it so effectively in "My Papa's Waltz," rather than through statements of contrast; and as with Roethke the tone is dependent on a wise humor.

But *Music from Home* is more varied than I have indicated. I have mentioned the reminiscential poems, but there are also the poems of adult involvement. You can call them "Now" poems, as the author does in titling Part II, without indulging in the triteness currently adhering to the term. These poems are immediate in their allusions and they have an immediate appeal. They exhibit a variety of attitudes—from passionate caring to satirical amusement to downright anger—and somehow you know it is always the same person speaking. This is so because McElroy writes out of a wholeness of spirit rather than out of her wounds. Perhaps the following passages will suggest something of her range and control:

> Breasts taut, your head in a straight run,
> We claim and proclaim with moist hips
> Until I nestle in the warm hairs of your belly.

*

I lie spooned against your long lean thighs;
you ask for love and kiss my answer
into laughing little syllables.

*

An axe-handle legged woman
remembers you, senate man
she doesn't want to subdivide
her pay check, hiding four coins
in a sock for rainy days

*

I have a black look that I like,
It is not a mask I put on.
A young look, it goes on below my legs
and does not freckle in the sun.

*

In the white of the world,
You live up front
And learn the measure of words.
One set for others, one for them.
So I whisper, "hey Home";
Call and raise their bluff.
We all wonder if it's black enough.

*

Fat white men with black cigars
Sisters hissing under puffy 'fros
Dap black pontificators in white cars
Roaring——together! together!
This music is freedom. . . yeah!

To a certain extent we live in a time of poetry substitutes. There are
many who believe poetry a fine thing if they don't have to let it seriously
engage their minds. For these people the hucksters market what passes
for poetry. It satisfies, narrowly, their demand for social significance or
for gutsy realism. It may even present a sort of minority report which,
while couched in scolding terms, ends up by easing lightly smitten
consciences. It hasn't much to do with poetry, and many of our popular

songs, another sort of poetry substitute, are in fact more meaningful. They are also more fun.

Happily, however, poetry itself thrives. There are poets who, like McElroy, know the difference between a substitute and the real thing and who don't cheapen their product to sell it. If you have picked up this book because you want to hear a woman sound off, or a black sound off, go pick up another book. If you want to read the work of a remarkably gifted American poet, who neither hides nor exploits her sex and color, I recommend these poems to you. I don't think you'll ever forget them.

ACKNOWLEDGEMENTS

Grateful acknowledgement is extended to the following magazines for permission to reprint the following poems: *Aisling* (summer 1975), for "Horoscope"; *Black Lines*, 2, No. 3 (1973), for "Sister Charity"; *Choice*, No. 7-8 (1972), for "Daughter" and "Whispers"; *december*, 13, No. 1-2 (1971), for "For My Children" and "Under the Oak Table"; *Epoch*, 14, No. 3 (1975), for "A Navy Blue Afro"; *Fragments, A Literary Review*, 16, No. 1 (1975), for "And When My Love calls. . ."; *Jeopardy*, 7 (1971), for "Neighborhoods" and "Rehearsal"; Jeopardy, 11 (1975), for "Educating the Coed"; *Mill Mountain Review*, 2, No. 2 (1975), for "Grandma's Girls"; *Mill Mountain Review*, 2, No. 3 (1975), for "The Dance" and "The Mechanic"; *Northwest Review*, 12, No. 2 (1972), for "Penny-Ante"; *Out of Sight* (September 1974), for "Music From Home"; *Out of Sight* (November 1974), for "What Women Think About"; *Poetry Northwest*, 12, No. 2 (1971), for "Half A Week" and "Sweet Anna Took Time"; *Poetry Northwest*, 13, No. 1 (1972), for "Visiting"; *Poetry Now*, 2, No. 1 (1975), for "Another Morning"; *Seneca Review*, 5, No. 1(1974), for "In the NATIONAL GEOGRAPHIC"; *South Dakota Review*, 9, No. 4 (1972), for "The End of Sisterhood" and "Skintone"; *South Dakota Review*, 9, No. 4 (1973), for "News Report"; *Sunday Clothes* (spring 1974), for "For the Cheerleaders of Garfield High"; *Wild Fennel* (spring 1971), for "Cats"; *Wormwood Review*, 2, No. 4 (1971), for "Happily Ever After" and "Try to Understand Papa."

Appreciation is extended to Houghton Mifflin Company for gracious permission to quote from Anne Sexton's poem "Again and Again and Again," which appeared in her volume *Love Poems* (Boston: Houghton Mifflin Company, 1967).

The following poems of Colleen J. McElroy are also reprinted herein from her volume *The Mules Done Long Since Gone*, copyright © 1972 by Colleen J. McElroy, reprinted by permission of the publisher, the Harrison-Madrona Center: "Amen Sister," "The Dance," "For My Children," "Gra'ma," "The Last Conversation," "The Mechanic," "Music From Home," "Never Again: Not for Anne Sexton," "Night People," "Passing for Black," "Penny-Ante," "Senate Man," "Sister Charity," "Sunrise Poems," "Try to Understand Papa," and "What You Say."

I

Then

Under the Oak Table

I sit crotch high
  Scenting the heavy fat
  Of my ancestry,
Hearing stories of the Lord
  And ditch niggers
Both coming in from the South.

The heavy oak of table legs
  Doubled in pairs
  By oak legs of Mama's sisters,
As I hide in a private jungle
  Viewing the underside
Of table and kin.

Subjects of sin are whispered,
  But my ears are large
  Under the shroud of legs.
Brother, never mentioned without
  His hooked nose,
Refuses an invitation to tea.

This time I'll count wooden legs,
  And try not to sneeze away
  Five reasons Uncle Roman's son died.
A spider chooses the wrong leg,
  And I prepare him for burial
As Brother's wife is inspected—blood will tell.

A dozen times in one afternoon
  They relive the deaths
  Of favorite sisters, Fannie and Jessie.
Fannie looked like Mama.
  Soda pop and peckerwoods
Come in all flavors, some too sweet.

Kidney stew and dumplings mingle
  With the smell of musk and oak.
  While Claudia, head hauncho,
Takes her seat. Don't ask her twice;
  The biggest sister of them all,
And Mama leads the yes chorus.

Gra'ma

Gra'ma was a little bit of a thing,
Full of spirits wandering
From an Alabama plantation to St. Louis.
Three on a match and a hat on the bed
Says the oldest will die.
She told me this at the age of five.
Her skin spoke of Chinese coolies
And overseers. Her face sang
Of Tanzania near Congolese waters,
Crocodiles running rapidly by
Gathering stones as a village screamed
Its death throes. That combination
Got her in the house when she was young;
Scrubbing, serving and suckling
Pink babies. Kept her there
Until 40 acres and a mule
Times a hundred kin freed her
With that long tall man
We came to love as Papa.
Set them near a Georgia swamp,
Pulling half a year's living
From the soil. He moved her north
Where she had a story for every day.
Told me: Listen close, child,
The world and the Lord are both profound.
When Papa died, her stories grew shorter;
She forgot which of those 40 acres
Could be mine or how many mules
You need to pull a plow.
When she finally saw my son,
She said: I guess the mules
Done long since gone.

Try to Understand Papa

Papa's not too hard to understand;
   he was just a man
With a hawkish face and long steps
Ending in feet that emptied puddles.
Kept his manhood locked inside
His fists so tight, they turned
Ashen black.

Papa's easy to understand,
   if you're a man
Who stands high watching white folks
Slide by the brewery stable where
He kept the horses fine. Standing
His ground as they pranced on the end
Of the lead; standing so tall
He needed a spear.

Papa was an easy man to understand
   even then—
When he was so gentle they called him boy,
And couldn't see the thin bolt of vein
Corded from shoulder to forearm. I pluck
The wet scent of frying meat and the scent
Of his hands from those mornings
When he helped me wake.

Grandpa was a man who posed
   in a Ford
With his jaw at right angles to the sun,
And even cousins called him Papa
'cause they could understand
How he held out through a card game
That lost the house. Then won it back
Playing kept woman against man.

Gossip tells that he paced
   before the doorway
Of a fourposter and counted eight times
Before he got a son—then spent
His manhood away from home.
But I smell the scent of his hands
And purse the lips he gave me.
He loved as a man;
It's not too hard to understand.

Sweet Anna Took Time

Snakes
shed skin,
a gentle thin
shell too tight for fit;
but ladies unfold.
Some bleed,
others find virginity
a state of mind.

Somewhere in the middle
of the war,
sweet Anna took time
east by northeast;
her buffle head
a seamless case of morals,
her slippery skin in smooth
black bulges
like the emerald and lime
shadows of sweet peppers.
A chambered vacuum.

Soft safe Anna
packed case after case
of bullets for the boys
who became men,
while Anna
became Sweet.

Somewhere in time,
the Allies invade
with case after case
of the dust she checked,
her velvet fingers flecked grey.
She sits facing east
in the light from these beaches,
the wire mesh window
shadows her face.
A setting for a folk opera.

Anna watches for the enemy
and listens to mama's drone.
The boy checks the beach
as the voice ticks on;
his fingers weep
and he creeps
through the mesh—
In one sweet hour
the battle is won.

In her net hose,
she hunkers
wet and sweet;
and when she packed for
nowhere
at war's end,
Anna could not be found.

So Sweet returned.
She keeps her bed
virgin clean
and patches her shell.
Somewhere in time,
her mind
snaps shut
with a final dry
popping sound.

Penny-Ante

The red queen flops
Face down; a jack follows,
Double timed,
As Daddy's fingers flip
For twenty-one.
Drinking and waiting
For the right combination
Of black and red.

He played war games for 21,
Joined when all that Black folks
Could find was army.
Believes in it too—
Career, he tells the neighbor boy;
Big Red One, spit brown, fatigue green.

His nostrils expand
Like black pearls. Hands
Like butterflies turn
The cards through space
Or brush lint that isn't there
From his bristly face.

He talks of mess cooks, stew
And spent shells in the same breath.
It's up to you to laugh or cry,
The telling is his wealth.
Those memories aren't the right color
For the local VFW.

A thin crack cuts through
Dull gold thumbnail stains.
He strokes the deck;
Black hand against black king.

Thinking of places
He has been. The time he made
Spec-3, gut-kicked a trooper
From Fort Wayne. Lost his eagle
All for a chance to die equal.

A greasy slide of scotch
Settles in his throat.
His voice swings
Each card into play.
Twisting sounds and aces,
Top sergeant all the way.

Ok, short time, dealer's choice;
He snaps the edge of a queen,
Six cards, all red—
Ace is high,
Deuce to seven can't win.
He calls them like the evening news

Calls serial numbers, casualties,
Heavy losses, injuries—
Like the one his buddy got
With an M-1 in back of a tank.
Left Daddy alone, waiting, drunk
On GI gin and red tape.

Grandma's Girls

Grandma's girls wait like Godot characters
You never see them chat over embroidery.
They carry gossip in croaker sacks
And stir slick niggers with their coffee.

They sit in varying shades.
Claudia, the oldest, is president.
Lemon yellow and bitter
She could've been born in Montana

Riding the range.
Spent years shaking Arkansas dust
From her bosom
Now she takes cabs to prove she's city.

Her sister, Jennie, is a redhead
But black to her soul.
Surgeons have removed all but her love,
First the ovaries, gall bladder, then the breasts.

Now they patch and caulk.
The youngest, Ruth, is Brother's girl.
Her broken toe makes her his patsy.
Claudia believes women are built to wait

Broad hipped but thin as a sharecropper's check.
She's the anchor, sucking her teeth
Clucking the family into place
And counting the monthly returns.

A Poem for Pussy

Headstart begins with baby buggy races down Ash Hill,
Pussy stands wet nosed
Counting fireflies in a jar.
Ain't got no abacus.
Mama's wash board leans in the hall,
A good morning exercise.

Pussy's at the store——coin wrapped in a crumpled note,
Old Man Farrow calls it hog-mogonized
But grown folks say it comes from cows.
That child just stands there——wondering.
Black shadows lead to the porch
Where Pussy's uncle sways out to nowhere;
Don't tell him he has fits.

Three times in the same grade,
Too early for new theories.
A long way from cotton fields to Headstart.
Mama doesn't understand——be careful, child.
So we jump Double-Dutch in the sun,
And Pussy, the best, stands by for her turn.

16

The Lesson

(for Claudia)

Six hours late,
Hopalong and Black Bart
rode four times that day.
(*But not as hard
as you, Big Mama*.)
Suck your teeth,
they're brand new.
No matter that they pull
your broad flat face
into an eternal grin,

You got the Lord on your side,
and me, in Brownie dress
and saddle shoes
straddling your words
like a jungle gym.
(*I'm a spider
rolled into a furry ball*.)

Lord, Lord, Big woman,
they double dog dared me.
I know
the WORLD IN NEWS AND SPORTS
ends the matinee.
But home is you,
arms akimbo,
crossing your bosom like swords.
Hoppy is timeless,
popcorn is better.

13

Next Saturday?
I'll be here forever
listening
to your off-the-wall words
ending
sharply and sharp
with a click of teeth.
Yess—no—I hear.
(*Your thighs are wrinkled*.)

Yeah, Yeah, Old Lady,
I know it costs a dime.
(*Your soul's so stingy*
it pocks your cheeks.)
But Hopalong's in pain
riding on the dry crackle
of your words.

I held his hat
clean and white,
a jerky, dusty
24 frames a second—
Black Bart,
cactus and ranches.
Then you,
in black and white.
(*A lot of yella*
gone to waste.)

Six

The year
Aunt Clara moved to
California
Papa got caught sellin
peppered feed at the b
Aunt Clara sent us a ɉ
no return address
Grandma never stoppe
buffalo fish while I reɛ
picture side first
she hummed a church
off-key and kind of loᵥ
like the tunes she sang
when I took sick
humming as she rubbe
the hot goose grease
then bound my chest
in cheese cloth
Brother wanted to see
a cougar in Yellowstor
so Papa drew a map
on the fogged up dinin
sketching in the road tᵢ
all that year I traced it
with my finger
counting the cities
and waiting for Papa tᵢ

Flushings

Having made the step from chamber pot
to porcelain bowl,
I remember the grey cracks,
long chains with pot bellied pulley.
You, the stump
beside the bandy leg tub,
one step
beyond the age of half moon doors.
Your figure is impressive,
never in disguise
though they change your mouth to a T,
and your waters run blue
to hide the private scents.

In my youth, you stood
down the cold end of the hall
and I took my relief
in a cloak of shivers.
Once, while Grandpa sighed,
I sneaked a glimpse of male parts.
Later, I stood with girls
of ten and twelve
facing long rows of your image
all white and two feet high.
Your smell, public;
our talk, sex
explored and exclaimed by word
of mouth
before your yawning maw.

Chin resting on wet rim,
forced by indulgence,
I shared my first booze with you.
Mop in hand,
six seconds after overflow,
I watched, oh fickle bowl,
as you returned the favor.

Babies are forced
to serve you.
Your sound brings a flush
of memory even to the rich.
You've never been
a gentleman.

Wooden seats that squeak,
bowls that sweat,
you've become old friend.
Greeting winter mornings,
sharing dirty books.
You bear the burden of my past.
We sigh in asthmatic chorus.
Each time I pray
for a light crescendo,
but you, dear john
rudely vocal, scream on
as once more
my system demands relief.

Webs and Weeds

Sidewalks of webs and weeds
Run parallel to empty lots where foul deeds
By handkerchief heads and winos were played,
To that old house where we stayed.
Irma Jean, Cora Jean and I, three debs,
Against the cracks of weeds and webs.

Sitting through matinees, dodging chores,
Chewing gum; claiming boys were bores.
But secretly grooming hair and breasts;
Jennie's brood, a female nest.
Irma, long legged, delicious full lips
Taught Cora and I to wiggle our hips.
George Darlington Love, a beau, my first.
They yelled his name like a tribal curse

As his virginal fingers pressed our bell.
Against that background of sights and smells,
We ignored switch blades, zip guns, and knees
Shattered by cops in that place without trees.
Now memories of dances are sprinkled like seeds
Among cousins and sidewalks of webs and weeds.

Neighborhoods

Mr. Charlie tells us niggers learn 12 blocks from Kennerly Avenue,
So we walk long rows of tavern smells.
Bumpsy and Pussy play Twenty-four Robbers;
The peckerwoods swing——fenced in,
And I kiss behind the ash pits the first time.

Kennerly lies straight and grey, a slash midway
the Black Belt at the mouth of the Mighty Miss.
The only green erupts in barbed clusters
Between the houses rising at a slant, a Gothic nightmare.
We watch dogs fight for a bitch in heat,

And learn to bet on the loser, sucking
Pickles and peppermint, a penny a piece at the Jew's.
In scarred wooden seats, our nappy heads nod
The tune of the anthem, but we dream on brick walls
Playing the Dozens with Charlie's mama.

Rosalind's brother is one Fifth Dimension,
Old Charlie pays to see him sing now.
I sit entombed with chalkboard and rules
Counting books——too old for pickles and peppermint,
But every nigger knows how far it is from Kennerly.

Sidewalk Games

I

The sidewalks were long where I grew up,
They were as veined as the backs
Of my Grandma's hands.
We knew every inch of pavement;
We jumped the cracks
Chanting rhymes that broke evil spirits,
Played tag at sunset
Among the fireflies and sweet maple trees
Or sang wishful sonnets about boyfriends
To the tune of whipping jump ropes.
The sidewalks wrapped around corners
Like dirty ribbons lacing the old houses
Together in tight knots;
Maple trees bordered
The all-white cemetery.
Sometimes we'd watch Priscilla's uncle
Sway down the dirt alley towards home.
We called her Pussy, called him
Crazy Max.
He was feeble minded and took to fits,
Barely making it from alley to pavement,
Loping down the street like a drunk.

We paced his jagged walk
Against tumbling tunes,
Taunting each pigeon toed footstep
With rhyme.
The boys   bolder, louder
The girls   tagging along
Braids flopping like twisted hemp,
Ending in brightly colored ribbons.
We turned our black faces into silence
When he finally made it home;
Watched him grope up the broken concrete stairs,
Clutch the wooden railing,
Lunge for the broken screen door
And his medicine.

His tongue flopped wildly,
Parrot noises drowning his sister's cries
As she rushed from the black pit
Of their house.

One day, he leaned away from the safe umbrella
Of his sister's voice;
Leaned into the sky,
Hanging on the porch rail like a rag doll,
Then fell into the cracks of the sidewalk.
We rarely chanted after that,
Always passed Pussy's house in silence.
Sometimes I'd sit in the sweet stillness
Of Grandma's moldy basement
And draw his outline on the wet fuzzy walls.
The grey concrete backdropped my stick figure.
As it fell into nothingness.

II

Bumpsy played the Dirty Dozens
As we jack-knifed the length of the block
Forcing grown-ups off the street.
We linked arms like soldiers,
Our black legs scissoring in precision.
   One's a company, two's a crowd
   Three on the sidewalk is not allowed—
   Last night, the night before
   Twenty-four robbers at my door— ·
   Po-lice, po-lice, do your duty
   Make this boy stop feeling my booty—
   Mary, Mary, tell me true
   Who is the one you love?
Tin soldiers, wooden guns, and sharp tongues.
We got comic books for the price of one
In blitz attacks at Old Man Farrow's dirty store.
Garages were secret places for dirty jokes,
Our folks couldn't afford cars.
When we got older, we played house for real
Until we found Terry's baby sister's body
Behind a stack of tires;
The melodies we'd sung still seemed to bounce

The Lesson

(for Claudia)

Six hours late,
Hopalong and Black Bart
rode four times that day.
(*But not as hard*
as you, Big Mama.)
Suck your teeth,
they're brand new.
No matter that they pull
your broad flat face
into an eternal grin,

You got the Lord on your side,
and me, in Brownie dress
and saddle shoes
straddling your words
like a jungle gym.
(*I'm a spider*
rolled into a furry ball.)

Lord, Lord, Big woman,
they double dog dared me.
I know
the WORLD IN NEWS AND SPORTS
ends the matinee.
But home is you,
arms akimbo,
crossing your bosom like swords.
Hoppy is timeless,
popcorn is better.

13

Next Saturday?
I'll be here forever
listening
to your off-the-wall words
ending
sharply and sharp
with a click of teeth.
Yess—no—I hear.
(*Your thighs are wrinkled.*)

Yeah, Yeah, Old Lady,
I know it costs a dime.
(*Your soul's so stingy
it pocks your cheeks.*)
But Hopalong's in pain
riding on the dry crackle
of your words.

I held his hat
clean and white,
a jerky, dusty
24 frames a second—
Black Bart,
cactus and ranches.
Then you,
in black and white.
(*A lot of yella
gone to waste.*)

Six

The year
Aunt Clara moved to
California
Papa got caught selling
peppered feed at the brewery
Aunt Clara sent us a postcard
no return address
Grandma never stopped scaling
buffalo fish while I read it
picture side first
she hummed a church song
off-key and kind of low
like the tunes she sang
when I took sick
humming as she rubbed in
the hot goose grease
then bound my chest
in cheese cloth
Brother wanted to see
a cougar in Yellowstone
so Papa drew a map
on the fogged up dining room window
sketching in the road to California
all that year I traced it
with my finger
counting the cities
and waiting for Papa to return

A Poem for Pussy

Headstart begins with baby buggy races down Ash Hill,
Pussy stands wet nosed
Counting fireflies in a jar.
Ain't got no abacus.
Mama's wash board leans in the hall,
A good morning exercise.

Pussy's at the store——coin wrapped in a crumpled note,
Old Man Farrow calls it hog-mogonized
But grown folks say it comes from cows.
That child just stands there——wondering.
Black shadows lead to the porch
Where Pussy's uncle sways out to nowhere;
Don't tell him he has fits.

Three times in the same grade,
Too early for new theories.
A long way from cotton fields to Headstart.
Mama doesn't understand——be careful, child.
So we jump Double-Dutch in the sun,
And Pussy, the best, stands by for her turn.

Flushings

Having made the step from chamber pot
to porcelain bowl,
I remember the grey cracks,
long chains with pot bellied pulley.
You, the stump
beside the bandy leg tub,
one step
beyond the age of half moon doors.
Your figure is impressive,
never in disguise
though they change your mouth to a T,
and your waters run blue
to hide the private scents.

In my youth, you stood
down the cold end of the hall
and I took my relief
in a cloak of shivers.
Once, while Grandpa sighed,
I sneaked a glimpse of male parts.
Later, I stood with girls
of ten and twelve
facing long rows of your image
all white and two feet high.
Your smell, public;
our talk, sex
explored and exclaimed by word
of mouth
before your yawning maw.

Chin resting on wet rim,
forced by indulgence,
I shared my first booze with you.
Mop in hand,
six seconds after overflow,
I watched, oh fickle bowl,
as you returned the favor.

17

Babies are forced
to serve you.
Your sound brings a flush
of memory even to the rich.
You've never been
a gentleman.

Wooden seats that squeak,
bowls that sweat,
you've become old friend.
Greeting winter mornings,
sharing dirty books.
You bear the burden of my past.
We sigh in asthmatic chorus.
Each time I pray
for a light crescendo,
but you, dear john
rudely vocal, scream on
as once more
my system demands relief.

Webs and Weeds

Sidewalks of webs and weeds
Run parallel to empty lots where foul deeds
By handkerchief heads and winos were played,
To that old house where we stayed.
Irma Jean, Cora Jean and I, three debs,
Against the cracks of weeds and webs.

Sitting through matinees, dodging chores,
Chewing gum; claiming boys were bores.
But secretly grooming hair and breasts;
Jennie's brood, a female nest.
Irma, long legged, delicious full lips
Taught Cora and I to wiggle our hips.
George Darlington Love, a beau, my first.
They yelled his name like a tribal curse

As his virginal fingers pressed our bell.
Against that background of sights and smells,
We ignored switch blades, zip guns, and knees
Shattered by cops in that place without trees.
Now memories of dances are sprinkled like seeds
Among cousins and sidewalks of webs and weeds.

Neighborhoods

Mr. Charlie tells us niggers learn 12 blocks from Kennerly Avenue,
So we walk long rows of tavern smells.
Bumpsy and Pussy play Twenty-four Robbers;
The peckerwoods swing——fenced in,
And I kiss behind the ash pits the first time.

Kennerly lies straight and grey, a slash midway
the Black Belt at the mouth of the Mighty Miss.
The only green erupts in barbed clusters
Between the houses rising at a slant, a Gothic nightmare.
We watch dogs fight for a bitch in heat,

And learn to bet on the loser, sucking
Pickles and peppermint, a penny a piece at the Jew's.
In scarred wooden seats, our nappy heads nod
The tune of the anthem, but we dream on brick walls
Playing the Dozens with Charlie's mama.

Rosalind's brother is one Fifth Dimension,
Old Charlie pays to see him sing now.
I sit entombed with chalkboard and rules
Counting books——too old for pickles and peppermint,
But every nigger knows how far it is from Kennerly.

Sidewalk Games

I

The sidewalks were long where I grew up,
They were as veined as the backs
Of my Grandma's hands.
We knew every inch of pavement;
We jumped the cracks
Chanting rhymes that broke evil spirits,
Played tag at sunset
Among the fireflies and sweet maple trees
Or sang wishful sonnets about boyfriends
To the tune of whipping jump ropes.
The sidewalks wrapped around corners
Like dirty ribbons lacing the old houses
Together in tight knots;
Maple trees bordered
The all-white cemetery.
Sometimes we'd watch Priscilla's uncle
Sway down the dirt alley towards home.
We called her Pussy, called him
Crazy Max.
He was feeble minded and took to fits,
Barely making it from alley to pavement,
Loping down the street like a drunk.

We paced his jagged walk
Against tumbling tunes,
Taunting each pigeon toed footstep
With rhyme.
The boys   bolder, louder
The girls   tagging along
Braids flopping like twisted hemp,
Ending in brightly colored ribbons.
We turned our black faces into silence
When he finally made it home;
Watched him grope up the broken concrete stairs,
Clutch the wooden railing,
Lunge for the broken screen door
And his medicine.

His tongue flopped wildly,
Parrot noises drowning his sister's cries
As she rushed from the black pit
Of their house.

One day, he leaned away from the safe umbrella
Of his sister's voice;
Leaned into the sky,
Hanging on the porch rail like a rag doll,
Then fell into the cracks of the sidewalk.
We rarely chanted after that,
Always passed Pussy's house in silence.
Sometimes I'd sit in the sweet stillness
Of Grandma's moldy basement
And draw his outline on the wet fuzzy walls.
The grey concrete backdropped my stick figure.
As it fell into nothingness.

II

Bumpsy played the Dirty Dozens
As we jack-knifed the length of the block
Forcing grown-ups off the street.
We linked arms like soldiers,
Our black legs scissoring in precision.
    One's a company, two's a crowd
    Three on the sidewalk is not allowed—
    Last night, the night before
    Twenty-four robbers at my door— ·
    Po-lice, po-lice, do your duty
    Make this boy stop feeling my booty—
    Mary, Mary, tell me true
    Who is the one you love?
Tin soldiers, wooden guns, and sharp tongues.
We got comic books for the price of one
In blitz attacks at Old Man Farrow's dirty store.
Garages were secret places for dirty jokes,
Our folks couldn't afford cars.
When we got older, we played house for real
Until we found Terry's baby sister's body
Behind a stack of tires;
The melodies we'd sung still seemed to bounce

Off the dirty walls and stacks of comic books.

III

Our houses ended at the sidewalk,
Whitewashed steps gleaming like teeth
Against the blocks of grey pavement.
We walked three blocks just to find
A vacant lot to feed Mildred's thirst
For green grass.
Fat Vaughn could eat a whole sheet
Of newspaper in less than three minutes.
Once, I licked the damp cellar wall,
But the taste didn't match the sweet smell.
Ten years later, I searched through Grandma's
Things before they were sold for auction.
I found her picture, three comics and the wind-up
Victrola we used to put on our version
Of Cotton Club musicals.
We traded days so we could all be stars;
The rest sang chorus until the Victrola
Ran out of steam, the record moaning
Like a sick calf.
I found the stack of old pillows
We collapsed on, giggling and tumbling
Against each other like puppies,
While the needle stuck in one groove
Cutting circles in the records.

Amen Sister

Amen sister fans the heat toward the Lord,
Virgin cotton dress, gloves, and hat in place.
Gloves whitewashed in cold water the night before.
Shoes shine shinola white;
A plastic purse hangs from her arm,
She carries the family history in her head.

Amen sister,
Your knees have kissed Miss Ann's floor all week,
But this day is yours. The girls are clean,
You've got the boys off the street,
Scrubbed and looking for the devil in every pew.
(He tempts you too, but not today,

Thank you, Lord.)
Your summer legs shine vaseline, sister.
Pattern hat of straw and flowers set straight.
You walk head on into the world today,
Holding yourself together at the waist,
Bosom blooming with each chorus.
Watch those boys, catch their eye,
And remind them of the wrath of the Lord.

Amen sister,
Fine preacher, so young;
Smile your sunday teeth, nod your head
In tune to the young people's choir.
The Man's not here today
To see your powdered face.
Your hands are busy with the work of the Lord.
Don't dust biscuits, talk to your people,
Speak in tongues, shout,
Sing of the troubles you have seen.
Amen, sister, amen.

The End of Sisterhood

Picking out words from beer stained funny papers,
Long before Lucy meets Peanuts,
Soon after See Spot Run.
Hope Brenda Starr finds that Masked Man.
Me, I don't need no man.

Old Man Farrow lies silent under the shed's broken roof,
His dog guards week old bread.
Grandma tells me which number to dial.
Then, I learn to wait for private calls
From boys with three part names.

Skin tossed black in the sunlight,
We walk grouped for protection.
Dresses hanging out of line
Searching for female places on willow bodies;
Smiling puppy dog smiles.

Leather jackets of tribal origin bedeck our crowd.
Young girls with knees locked against grace
Search each other with butterfly kisses,
Buds of new breasts erect; I abstain in disdain,
But that was before I found Dutch Red
Too sweet for my blood.

Long after Papa sat high in his '29 Ford
With Uncle Lewis' wife in a summer hat,
I count minutes in the back seat of a '49,
Watched as I race for calls no longer private.
How many sisters you got, Mama?
Claudia counts for two.

The smell of sandlot dirt and sound of blue jean zippers
Ends one final groping, ends sisterhood.
Nothing ventured, nothing gained.
So I bang into full bloom
Stunned by pain.

Coupled and recoupled, I sit counting drops of sweat,
Passions shared with my old used-to-be's.
Seersucker, dotted swiss, See Jane See Dick
Now they're all together, sweet young things,
Papa, Brenda Starr, and Old Man Farrow.

Recess

I come here alone   standing wet
and poetic in the rain
the school is still the same
dusty windows reflect dogs
stuck inside a chain link fence
bricks smoothed by a thousand
tennis shoes and slamming doors
dull glass squares hide
rooms full of radiator smells
windows like checkered eyes
defying truants
in Sioux City, Biloxi, and St. Louis
I watch from the playground
and play out memories
each ghost a marble in my game
my new suede boots sound hollow
clumsy on these quick stones
I haunt friends

ten of us run blindly for a swing
kick a loose ball rolling by a line
of second graders   we're older, wise
even wiser now there's only six
four of us died
comics in a war for Captain Kidd
the rest prayed
stood in front of open graves
in wispy groups
like in the fifth
where we warbled long division
that the veins of my hands remember
when I lift a wine glass
to toast Virginia's last baby
her tenth   he lays too quiet in the crib
she stands as before
head leaning slightly to the side

at ten that pose would hide
pigtails as she stood at the board
wandering through prose rules
for saying things just so
she married Harry
always falling off his seat
smelled of unwashed socks
still does   smelled even worse
when he was shot by a cop

it's all there under the chalk dust
the Elmer's glue   x sum squared
and sandwiches stuck to wax paper
today's big dealer
sits between another war's hero
and a mother of ten
he picks his nose   she watches
the rain fall in wet strings
out there where I stand
wet   smoking   thinking poet
thinking   smoking in the rain

Rehearsal

I

She comes to the wall
hair in a bun
on the back of her head
like a tit.
I'm yours for 2 coppers
cries the wall,
but she writes for the love of Paris
in words that wheeze and whinny.
A doggerel
etched in comic relief
above her line
brings joy
to the loveless souls
of men
who come to scrawl
along the wall.
Their words flung like spit balls
falling and sliding
into cracks
sniffed by large dogs.
Her ass bulges
like the belly of the oud
played nightly
at the bathkeeper's house.

She bends
toward the wall, her toga pulled
taut
scratching her one line love
for the eyes of Pompeii.

II

She watches as pitch
seals the bark
of the gong. Black
hands

mark the spot for the slit
of the great drum.
In a tight pause
between beats,
the drum glows
with the blood of a young boy;
then gossip travels
in wayward words that gather
force in space
before they shatter to the floor
of the Tiv or Luba.
Her feet peck the dust
in a rhythm
that the drum
will take in 2 tone words,
to call sorrow or war
and her love for
Ndugu.
A rivulet of sweat
traces the curve of her breast
and she calls the drum by name.

III

Her boots beneath the bed,
she prints
this poem in a neat
strong hand
with borrowed triangles
of used sounds
from a dead silent wall
or a royal drum.

Half A Week

Monday I awoke with a case
of the uglies.
Skin burlaped across my chin,
my cheeks were ungainly dunes
of black lava
absorbing cream without recognition.
I sat in the mirror,
A Madison Avenue conjure woman.

Tuesday I walked around
inside myself all day.
Looking out, I never saw
my face.
Met a man who knew 16 shades
of white
but only a single shade
of black.
He tried fitting me
with several blonde wigs;
and in the mirrored light
of his eyes,
my image grew duller and duller
until finally, he disappeared.

I gave up Wednesday to a woman
with a cinnamon slash of lips
and pure genes.
Just donated the whole day
intact, like her hymened thoughts.
She comes from good stock
and when she comes
it is with breeding, culture,
and money.
That sphincter of a mouth
assured the world of birth control.

Thursday I covered myself
with words.
Situation hung from my left shoulder,
and delight brushed the insides
of my thighs.
I plucked black mood
from the hair of a blonde
and hung it from my breasts.
Though I truly searched,
I couldn't find anything decent
to give her in return.

The Mechanic

(for J.B.)

Tires are blackbirds on the rack,
His hands are black
Against the thin dimes he clanks
Into the till.
His daughter's ill and young son
Already gone bad.
Eyes set yellow in puffy black cheeks;
Jeans slack in the ass, stained
Like a Chevy truck.
He coughs into the dust
Of a rebuilt engine;
Not sure which one will die first,
Or finally.
He died ten years ago
When a purple haired counselor
Tracked him into vocational high.
Artist hands are now
Grooved beyond repair;
Artist mind gone dull.
He counts valves,
Pumps gas;
Trying to remember
The texture of tempura paints.

Mother

When you pushed me forward and over
in your twilight sleep
your regal Eritrean nose
twitched
like a deer in shock
your black thighs flexed
and grew oily with blood
the smell reached through
your sedated night
your temples pulsed like the moss
canopy of a disturbed underbrush

only when your sweat grew cold
did you sing aloud
one final song for the impala
I was late
unwilling to abandon your comfort
you dreamed of emerald green forests
where you floated beautifully
among the waxy leaves
running swiftly
like a wedge of black light
queleas and touracos
singing to your run

I used to watch you dream
your temples pulsing to woodwinds
the light across the bridge
of your nose angling
towards some equatorial place
where plump fruit falls ripe
for your taking
I watched trying to remember
the comfort of your womb

today I remembered
your song
sat in the easy chair
humming softly
as my children
watched me

Daughter

words trill on the tip
of your tongue

the squeak of a hummingbird

nothing major
all in a minor key

the dove paces on a pulse beat
of coos

your breath hangs suspended
like the flutter of wingtips
against the sun

a parrot screams
in the green distance

you sit in a browner shade

a mixture of fine tea
ooling, ginger and anise

your face holds the mystery
of a night safari

your smile
the quiet waters of halcyon days

you wash my thoughts
in taffy

standing fast on spindly legs
a heron is caught in the shadows
of Africa's hills

a player piano sings
in your throat
set to the tune of tiny bells

bronze
like the palms
of your hands

For My Children

I have stored up tales for you my children
  My favorite children, my only children;
Of shackles and slaves and a bill of rights.
But skin of honey and beauty of ebony begins
  In the land called Bilad-as-Sudan,
So I search for a heritage beyond St. Louis.

My memory floats down a long narrow hall,
  A calabash of history.
Grandpa stood high in Watusi shadows
In this land of yearly rituals for alabaster beauty;
Where effigies of my ancestors are captured
  In Beatle tunes,
And crowns never touch Bantu heads.

My past is a slender dancer reflected briefly
  Like a leopard in fingers of fire.
The future of Dahomey is a house of 16 doors,
The totem of the Burundi counts 17 warriors—
  In reverse generations.
While I cling to one stray Seminole.

My thoughts grow thin in the urge to travel
  Beyond Grandma's tale
Of why cat fur is for kitten britches;
Past the wrought iron rail of first stairs
  In baby white shoes,
To Ashanti mysteries and rituals.

Back in the narrow hallway of my childhood,
  I cradled my knees
In limbs as smooth and long as the neck of a bud vase,
I began this ancestral search that you children yield now
  In profile and bust
By common invention, in being and belonging.

The line of your cheeks recalls Ibo melodies
    As surely as oboe and flute.
The sun dances a honey and cocoa duet on your faces.
I see smiles that mirror schoolboy smiles
    In the land called Bilad-as-Sudan;
I see the link between the Mississippi and the Congo.

A Poem Is

A cushion for a spongy head
A maze to map the brain
Alliterative lines to relive
The past like Daddy's thick 78
Recordings of Nellie Lutcher
In her prime
Like Daddy drunk and boasting
On his WW II ribbons lying
Next to his court-martial papers
A knife that cuts
The world's terror
Like lemon wedges and fits
It thinly between words
Even lonely poems are crowded
Ideas become anger
Moving slowly like clouds
Like mucus in your sinuses
Captured and potent
Like whiskey on the rocks
Even old love affairs
Become obscure references
In a poem

Horoscope

I am the October lady
Destined to live and die
In the first 31 days of fall
I have more in common
With my lover's wife
Than with my lover
We float on the same sun sign
Check the Libra message
Watch us serve love/hate
Anger for breakfast
She is my sister
This will become
Increasingly clearer
Check Gemini and Aquarius

I am the intruder
Shaded, I curl tight
My sting kinked into
A black decimal point
I am zero, potent or helpless
Fused to an invisible screen
Hiding my head in its folds
Like one of Pablo Neruda's
Fantastic birds
Like the aril of a bittersweet
Time is on my side
My images of you are grotesque
I am devious and tantalizing
Let me help you wander
Through star sign, sun sign
Through orchestrations of planets
Lie low, act accordingly
You will know what I mean.

II

Now

Music from Home

A four string bass
plays into the heart
of the rain forest.
Pure black sound,
moving sound—
Ngoma— Ngoma—
stirring snakes and ladies
of warrior tribes.

The deep wet sound
calms an echoing drum
as it rocks through the jungle.
It's a train— wheels smoking,
engine plowing through a dark
green night. I swallow
the sound, become passenger,
driving myself through the depths
of the train. Ngoma— I am oil.

My toes are dry and itch
to move, my hips to bend.
I plunge into a second skin,
glisten like the burnt case
of the walnut fiddle.
The cowbells are my feathers.
The drummer's hand paints my face.
Ngoma— I am bush woman.

Halfway home, my palm sings
as the bass player
plucks a blue moan
driving forty camels
into Timbuktu,
salt slabs and sweet
berry wine. Ngoma—
I sip from the only glass
in town.

In the NATIONAL GEOGRAPHIC

Follow the rays of the sun
Going down
To a line of trees
Holding shadows
Of man and woman
Look closely at sandy soil
Scrub brush holds their imprint
See them clearly

His touch is all that's left
His feet are bony, black
Flat as mine
Clumps of sand stick
Between his toes where shadows
Of his spear fall
Hiding a scorpion
Or a twig that stuck
During his last trip south

Look closer
She stands beside him
Her long lean fingers
Wiping dampness from her thighs
Her full lips are ironwood black
Parched and partly open
Her ears hear you even now

Stare at me
And watch his nostrils flare
Watch her shoulder turn as I leave
Notice how our faces glisten
Darkly in the sun. His mark
Is on my forehead. Her fingers
Wove the shallows of my collar bone
My feet remember the heat of Africa
Last night they told me
How to hunt the jackal

What Women Think About

a new man, no name
the body a melting weight
you think of
fresh mint love
fig sweet love
beyond the Song of Solomon love
daydreams for strangers
wicked and wise
wonderous as treasures
laid bare by shifting African deserts
you try saying it casually
even neutral words
are powerful as megatons
tested at White Sands
and you
frail as the safety
in Eden's apple

his profile
curve of mouth
strong thighs
all add up to fine silk love
chiffon with strong perfume
thick sweaty armpit love
pungent honey sweet
cleansing and filling the pores
what few words you find
are whispered songs
erotic woodwind notes
with a few secret phrases
in Geez and Runic
that leave you mute
he walks into tomorrow
where another planet burns
the feeling goes with him
leaving you
and your memory
clicking like the change
in your coin purse

Night World

At night, I listen to your real world;
steady thump, discordant sound or two
pressing my right ear.

My cheek against your furry chest;
our cold feet make us Sasquasch—
twin headed night creature.

Your even breathing, my wheeze;
and a thundering cave.
I crank my ear

Tuning the spiral inside to treble;
checking the tweeters,
checking the sounds you hide by day

Under your gambler's hat
and turtle neck shirts.
What goes on in there?

A rusty nail, bent and scraping bone?
A feather boa left by some Minnesota
flame, rustling in lonesome song?

I can recognize sounds
from clear around the world;
buildings clanking into life,

Machine guns spitting into swamps
as alligators die for a spring purse,
or tattered sheets

On rusted wire clotheslines
behind the White House.
I can hear thunder; I know water.

Liquid colors expand, disappear
like jewels on the waves;
the oil slick's a mermaid's coat.

I hang on to life;
squeezing jelly with my fingers
as I slide in darkness between stars.

You there, in your cave,
are you warm or white
as the day you stepped on the kitten?

When you comfort me at night
as I lie in my vacuum of space,
do you ever watch me in surprise
inside your universe?

Whispers

Our Sunday talk perfumed,
 You ease in;
The bath becomes black and white and white again,
 A private lotion we both enjoy.
Loins covered, pillows fluffed,
 My muff stays warm.
The oompah rhythm begins and gains.
The language varies like characters in a dance,
 I follow, you lead, you follow—
Devoted to the frequency of turns.
 Breasts taut, your head in a straight run,
We claim and proclaim with moist hips
 Until I nestle in the warm hairs of your belly.

And when my love calls...

I am the ocean
lost in deserts and canyons
I have no time for fear
I am evil and moody
only in your mind
Snails smooth my hair
Fish and witches are friends
I am dark, first satin
then velvet, catching light
only in shallows
My skin is smooth
dressed in warm sparkles
A gift from my love
He is the sun
His smile brilliant
His hair a tangled mass
A thick ring that filters
light, giving light
letting the shadows
Of his shoulder lie upon me
I rise to the shadows
My body arched and laced
in froth. He brushes
Seaweed from my legs
I crash against rocks
and running under the heat
of his love, I forget
become power, causing
Dar es Salaam to seek shelter
We move together
sighing and falling
past Barbados and Georgia
Locked in rhythm
we lie spent
rocking gently south of some shore
When my love cools, I am calm
and work again to move plankton
toward Alaska in the night

Each day my love is new
I meet him somewhere near Libya
lose him near Alkai Point
Each night, I search for him
among the rocks
checking footprints in the sand
Still warm from his laughter.

Sunrise Poems

Sunrise: Spring

In the hollow of a tree between the branches,
a tiny flower waits for the sun. Butterflies keep score,
their wings shedding colors that fold and unfold.

Between his fingers and the hollows of his palms,
man creates his world. His joys counted by the number
of fingers, folding and unfolding.

Mapped in the hollows of my head and thighs,
your memory flows in water colors. A multitude
of prints—some spread, some nested in folds.

You pillow my head in the hollow of your arm;
set the table for a feast and inviting a thousand
candles, your tender fingers remember every fold.

Between your lips, I live within the hollows
of your mouth. My joys counted by the number
of kisses and coming fast, I fold and unfold.

Sunrise: Summer

Bees buzz for nectar;
cicadas and dragonflies claim their death
in dry lightning snaps against the front door.

Yellow lace screens honeysuckle light
through each pane of fly-specked glass.

A sail-plane shimmers in Lummi's hot updraft
before it's sucked soundless into the mudflats.

We search for a cool breeze,
lying like beached whales in our own waste.

53

Night's cape is short. Summer's glare begins
with an early dawn and your touch.

Your voice nuzzles my ear;
your lips, my skin. I dance on your fingertips
and kiss a drop of sweat from your neck.

Sunrise: Fall

The first winds to turn cool
knife bone deep carrying the scent of wool.

The apples are finally ripe. Flapping wings
triangle the sky travelling south.

Mornings soon become
the crunch and clash of early frost
and first grade lunch pails.

But now the wind is wrapped in spice and gold
with shaded green beds for pumpkin, gourd
and pomegranate.

I lie spooned against your long lean thighs;
you ask for love and kiss my answer
into laughing little syllables.

I share your love and count summer's fading
freckles on each shoulder.

Sunrise: Winter

Kitchen spiced country light
washed green on oatmeal mornings.

Trees stand in a cold translucent fog,
a county-wide clothesline of dripping dungarees.

The bay glows gun-metal grey between log floats
where loons bob in soundless harmony.

Gulls battle headwinds, white rim of wing tips
against Lummi dyed lilac.

A ketch throws a shadowed triangle
adrift on the saffron sunrise.

I awake to the smooth lines of your back,
profiled in the soft cast of light. Beneath
the extra quilt, a new day begins.

Skintone

I can tell you a lot about skin,
tho' I've never been hung nude
above a bar
or in a gallery beside a blushing
Gainsborough.
Most of my skin watching
is in the bath
when it shrivels in the heat—
a peek at old age;
or pulls shiny tight and chalky white
in the snapping cold of winter
when lips become an elastic band.
I watch the patch of innocence
that lies hollowed above my collarbone,
a tender valley of sable
that blushes for no man;
or trace a high gloss
across the tip of my nose
or flat against my forehead.
I arch my back
against the grain of light
that shadows the hollow
along the ridge of my spine;
or watch a satin glow move
across the curve of my hip,
down my thigh,
and change black to caramel
as I pass a mirror.
But who wants to hear this song?
I'll go away and sigh alone,
and when my breasts rise on inhale—
they will billow
like ebony coverlets
across all Montana's hills.

Data: Age at Time of
Maximum Creativity

Out of studies
about black stupidity
chromosones percentaged
genes computed by color
I flip pages
to find Lehman's face
in chart form
rating creativity and age
telling me I'm too old
to write this damn poem

Lehman, do you mean to say
(roughly translated)
that creativity comes with youth
do you really mean to separate the years
by fives and chart my prime
chart my poetry by category
in my case, don't you think
you should divide each age
by color handicap
fancy that chart of yours
in fractions
each section squared
for the strain of segregation,
acculturation, genocide,
and possible cases of miscegenation

lyrics and ballads from 25–30
another five years for comedy
ending at 40 in philosophy
then on to cantatas
ignore the company you keep
schedule your life by this sheet
ignore the days you can't write
because your hands are oily
and the pen doesn't slide smoothly
the random days when taxes and booze
lay waste to thoughts

Lehman, you say I'm of the age
to move to bigger things
like tragedies or more specifically
hymns, but I want my glory before 40
complete with movie rights
you've fixed your rate in myth
it jerks me from the reality
of bigotry and bad weather
from children screaming
outside my window
from decisions of identity
from the desire to kill
my neighbor's Muzak

Senate Man

grey temples, tailored suit
contact blue eyes
we remember you, senate man
your square chin
jutting out for change
changing the way things have been
change for people oppressed
change for your pockets
and vest watch purchased in foreign markets
senate man, can you see
the faces in the mob
we fight to touch your sleeve
touch your mind
is your speech so refined and packaged
that you won't change
a single line to soothe the crowd
you've got the formula
you remember the words
turgid with just a dash of hope
you keep your senate place safe
in the roped-off section
groom your precincts and staff
with just enough class and race distinction
to span both right wing and left
good, not too deep
like the cleft in your chin
and your hands
just rough enough for making friends
we'll remember
what you said when the campaign ends

an axe handle legged woman
remembers you, senate man
she doesn't want to subdivide
her pay check, hiding four coins
in a sock for rainy days
planting the rest
up and down the block

her black hands dealing coins
to landlords, jew stores, numbers
and the First Baptist Ladies Aid
she wants to know, senate man
when she'll find a dime for the good life
like the one you keep
promising, real cream
and two weeks at the Hilton pool
fooling around with stocks and bonds
a black boogie remembers you too
a mantan coon daydreaming
about revolution
trying on his power tam
exercising his trigger finger
flexed four years ago for Uncle Sam
he's wondering how far
he can push your acceptance speech
the promises you said you'd keep
once in office
your smooth mouth
can't reward him, senate man
words licking across the microphone
as you wing toward a fifty dollar luncheon
forgetting

Consider

Find a web, a gauze of dust in the corner
Roll it between your fingers
Will certain colors allow a man to live longer?

Consider
The size, the span of the universe
Consider the question of color
When church was sky and earth.

Urban Poem

Outside my window
Tires eat the road
Growling as they chew
Spinning dirt through the air
Like saliva
The small grains of rubber
Have filtered into this poem.

Winters

(acrostic)

*W*alking hypnotic as a lion
   in the splendor of a 5 X 10 cage
*I*ce, mist and horizon
   mix with migraines and crusted soil
*N*othing grows but the children
*T*he timing's all wrong, details are dead still
   and vivid as a Breughel dream
*E*arth ends among the lilies,
   falling out of mind
*R*ooms grow smaller, hostile
   as you wait for the alien gold of sun
*S*addened by an ingrown toenail
   you limp toward some distant point.

Cats

MaMa Cat

Ill tempered bitch,
I've seen your kind before.
Feline outlines against watermelon
Smells of fresh cut grass.
Minx, Persian, tiger or crazy calico,
All leaving a fur flecked trail.

Your deaf ears, albino pink,
Rebound the calls for MaMa Cat.
You walk in a soundless world;
Asshole erect, an asterisk decoration
For periscope tail.

Quick to anger when I approach
Your blind side,
Your need for love is just as quick
And you purr about my legs,
Like a cockroach against bare skin.

Walking a nightly post past my door,
You tune your howls in a dead tympani;
Emitting screeches that shatter
Passion or sleep,
A pale shadow of your larger kin.
Eyes in a vertical pose—
One blue, one green; you stare
And I contemplate your inscrutable wisdom.
Then you eat a bug, wash toes and twat
With equal abandon.

I know your kind. Pretending your worth
By guarding the sunlight.
Sardonic grin and chipmunk cheeks
That frame a triangle of meows.
Scream your defiance, pink-lipped
Hare-lipped bitch.

I know you're watching me,
Even as you walk away;
Your legs jointed like ink
Spilled across a printed page.
Each pace set for a stage
Show or revue; just so
Prim you are and stylish, too
I like the rings
Centered on your hide,
But the best thing
Is your quiet meows
Not like the howls of your MaMa,
Honored bitch. Your cries
Are as smooth as your fur.
Nothing seems to bruise your mood,
Could it be those tubes
We tied a month or two ago?
You like to play patty-cake
With spiders,
None too small or too thin.
Then, when you're tired,
You eat them;
Stalking your prey like Gunsmoke.
Hey Kitty, I'll give you a dime
To call Doc and Chester
When you have the time.
Your coat by custom,
Your smile, Nefertiti;
Oh pretty Kitty, your owlish
Eyes are olives in a martini.

Never Again: Not For Anne Sexton

Lust has taken plant in it
and I have placed you and your
child at its milk tip.

I have a black look that I like,
It is not a mask I put on.
A young look, it goes on below my legs
And does not freckle in the sun.
A rich warm hue that needs no encouragement.

There is a look I wear on occasion,
A cape of whiteness that sits on my lips
And defecates establishment. I have tried
To put it on quietly. I paint it neutral,
The smoky grey of city faces, sewing it on
Each morning; but lust has taken plant in it
And I must eat.

Sometimes I take a good look
At what I must wear and cut it up
In a dozen pieces. I pour forth
In a rhythm that your bloodless kind
Can never know. The feel of cool breeze
Moves purple and brown and auburn
And black again as my face follows limbs
In a flash. The sweet feel of blackness
Comes as murderous relief and your milk tip
Is no more.

Passing For Black

I'm Jo, the Conju woman,
The boy Brother wanted.
One step Monday, the next Friday;
Every day a jangle
Of months. They're AKA
Moving cool a few steps away.
Tri-Delt Greeks in black face.
We'll cross at angles.

Stiff under my halfway grin,
I've been in this world
Too long, friend.
The changes blow cold,
The foxes close in.
Elbows nudge, eyes roll;
They check my 'fro,
My hair stands sponge cake tall.

Their tongues coil.
Those sister's vibes strike loud
Against the walls. Sounding
On my poor soul.
Twelve steps, my ears glow.
I step on a crack
And think
Of Brother's hooked nose.

The sun is gold as all
The bananas Brother ate
Before he got a stomach ache
In a 1949 tent.
He got the bicarb Gra'ma sent,
And Mama's lemon.
I'd like to run
But wet my lips and move on.

Box ankles roll past
Like pale poles swaying.
The sisters laugh,
Their earrings swing like targets.
I zero in on walnut faces.
They stare at Conju Jo
And pass without a sign.

In the white of the world,
You live up front
And learn the measure of words.
One set for others, one for them.
So I whisper, 'hey Home';
Call and raise their bluff.
We all wonder if it's black enough.

Visiting

The last time I went there, faces
Screamed from their tight shells.
The door opened half a space
To let my foot slip
In. I dread the trip.
I read my lines till I know them well.

There are bruises on the house,
Eyes that see neither night
Nor gloom. Mouse
Teeth in crocus skulls
Contrast my own in full
Relief. The lights are bright.

I'm veiled, my face a map
For their confessions.
My fingers pray in my lap.
"RighT ON", they say. "Righ'on", I reply.
My lips pucker on that lie.
Tips of fingers in obscene contemplation.

They stand in pairs, alone,
Beating their lamp shade skins.
Pink patrons: matrons,
A cover-girl, a jockey, a crone.
And I hand out pardons
For some of my best friends.

Happily Ever After

Princess, do you snore
Midway dreams of Disneyland,
Or will a cinder touch your eye
As you descend like Mary Poppins
To the edge of reality?
Were you conceived in blushes
At the Spring Prom,
Or did you begin
As a once upon a time girl?

Princess, do you sweat,
As you count your scents
And brush your hair spun gold
From drugstore potions?
Undies matched as carefully
As your placemats,
You part your maidenhair
And guard your maidenhead.

Princess, do you fuck,
Or wait for singular love
From a charming prince?
To you a cock must crow,
Dick is a first name
And aphrodisia a spray-on.
You rewrite recipes;
Raise your chest in hope,
But your hands are cold ——eyes afraid.

The pill is only sugar, princess;
Your trembles will aid the cause.
Stiff upper lip, old girl.
Practice the magic
Of words like yes and come.
Go wash your bush,
Fluff your pillow
And live happily.

Snow White in Aliceland

The drive-in fills with ducks at noon,
With tortoise and with hare.
Mirrors of the P.T.A. and soap opera set;
Madame La Farge and Marie Antoinette.
Sitting round, minds closed round
As wedding rings and coffee stains.
Suburbia's La Farge, girdled and staunch;
Mouth as tight as her morals
Under hollow eyes, slate grey.
Supermarket Antoinette, a pompadour
Of hair curlers and net bunting,
Changing detergents faster than ideas.
Nerve worn with consciousness,
Afraid I'll move next door,
They march on anything
In the name of virtue.

In the cylinders of napkins,
Silver images of ducks appear—
Children of the tortoise and the hare.
Who would marry those little white ducks,
Eyes focused for video? A programmed group,
Swinging on an ad man's okay;
They soap, spray, and twitter
In white tenny runners, so coo-well.
Still unweaned, groping for catsup and coke,
Through frosted hair, they whine.
Is it true they have more fun
Following those perfect mating patterns?
Poor little ducks. They want the good things,
Give them the right things,
Only the best things.

Sister Charity

Standing with the brothers
talking shit and swapping spit,
I see you roll past, sister,
crusading for poverty;
out of habit
and still a nun with the world.
Your feet flitter in and out of mod shoes
and pant suits,
but you still walk in holy attitude.
Next they'll put you on a stamp.

Shoulders straight, chin tucked in,
you pivot on your hands
peering under an invisible cap.
It's all done with mirrors,
a sleight of hand,
a dream, like I had when devoted
and thought of being spread
on a cross.

Of course, it is unchanged,
I fight the cross and double-cross,
your dream remains.
The brothers know
we each play a different game.
You're jiving, sister;
out of habit, you're still a nun,
singing faithful songs off-key,

All for the sake of charity.
You turn like a nun,
pale as an oyster's shell,
neck stiff from habit,
face composed, legs crossed;
talking about poverty like it's heaven's
blessings and the brothers are saints.
Ain't it time you looked at the world
without a hood?

It's not covered in your missal, sister,
you got to have soul
if you're gonna walk cold down
those mean streets.
Out in that bitter air,
your angel hair and fake wine
won't have time to work
before the deal goes down.

Prayers are the company you keep,
but Jodie's got your beads
in the street.
He thinks his mother's superior
to you. Shape up, sister,
don't you know we ALL live
in black and white?
We can't lose our vision from habit
and see your sabbath world.

Pike Street Bus

Poem, we're going this way,
With that bus,
Its driver fat and full
Of unspent words like you.
Tell them about it, poem.

It starts this way,
A slow lumbering thing
Turning the corner.
Then the lead line drops.
The bus is stuck like
The driver's face
In the rear view mirror
As he watches sparks dance
In front of Pike Market,
Watches the line throw fire.
The broccoli's put away,
Apples gone, fish face sideways
In neat rows under a layer
Of white paper.
There's heavy breathing
On the bus.

The driver's face is swollen,
The grey evening settles
In lines around his mouth.
His belly peeks out, dull white
Where a missing button
Lets his shirt stand open.
He leaves the bus, catching sight
Of the lead line hanging
Toward the broken pavement.
A few faces turn to watch;
Others look sideways.
She stares straight on,
Her black face tired,
Her arms remembering forty offices,
Mop handle imprints still cling
To her palms. Her eyes are old
Before her time.

Say it for her, poem.
Tell her dreams of places
Where she's always young,
Smiling and sitting straight
Like the picture that stares out
From her dresser. She's crisp;
Caught by the camera alive,
In love, not knowing this night,
This bus.

Ignore the drunk that staggers on,
Lurching toward the coin box.
He hangs at an angle
Against Seattle's fading sun.
He leans back, falling
Into his past, using his coins
For balance before diving
For the slot; a handful
Of attention on his face
As the change drops.

Plunging toward a seat
Smashing against her feet
And dreams, his mind leaves
Him once again. She rubs
Her cleaning woman knees,
Stroking toward the pain on the floor.
Extra fat on her chin bobbing
As she remembers how she last saw
Her man; sitting barefoot
Atop a kettle drum, pounding
At an eight hour day.

A Navy Blue Afro

I see her crossing the square
her hair
     glinting like the midnight
     of a blue Jamaican sky
she walks through the crowds
of ragged students
     her hair oddly blue
     her chin arched and poised
walking like some illustrated page
of today's woman
     you have seen them
     in their Rhine wine sunglasses
vying for visibility
     for cover stories
you have seen them
all those fake Furies
     coiffured
       powdered
         and costumed
their Medusa hair tamed
and dressed in new money
     they are so rich
     they piss in droplets
or fake it   commenting
in cultured voice on the latest trivia
     smiling   always smiling
     into the camera
you have seen them   poised
and ready for a call to charity
     microsex
       unisex
        jetsex
sometimes I can almost see
the girl with the navy blue hair
     among them
     until she turns
and her blackness sings to me
like a Jacob Lawrence painting.

What You Say

white folks always sitting around

comparing their knots
my left ball is Czechoslovakian
my right one is Hungarian

ever hear any black folks say
my left breast is Bantu
on my mother's side
my right one is Masai

white folks always asking

how do you do it
do you prefer the missionary position
have you tried anal innovation

ever hear any black folks ask
what do you think of vaginal orgasm
I rely on cerebral spasm

white folks always arranging

arranging special meetings to consider
talking about the Problem
wondering if they should ask

black folks to attend
what they want black folks for
no matter what the problem

they still talk about
Czechoslovakian missionary orgasms

The Last Conversation

Listen, I said,
rocking to the tingle in my spine,
At least try some other way
to change my mind.
Why not say we're both specks
in the universe,
tell me how our love is transparent
like clouds above the earth.
Let your tongue glide
like gulls swaying on updrafts.
Don't toss your words like sewage
spilled from a passing barge.
   I shouted this into the wind,
   green as his eyes
   as he turned, having said
   only, that he was leaving.

I'm cold, I said,
and tired of this put down world,
this light caught in a corset of time.
Working roots and conjure men,
juju all the way from Arachuku.
How can I walk with you on my back
telling me I'm all honey and wine
that needs no perfume and refined love?
   I screamed this into his hair,
   tight and black as gusts of night
   beat and churned
   by a silent owl's wings.
   He showed his teeth, smiling——Sister,
   he said, you have the power in your hands.

I ran, into the wind
shouting into a blonde crowd.
Told them how I've stared at my soul
so long, my eyes are naked,
lips hang loose as a trench coat
on a mad man exposing himself
to their tired words. They booed,
sang——hail to the chief,
god bless this land!
   They dined on a breakfast
   of peaches and cream, fasted
   for the poor on olives and caviar
   as the setting sun
   turned the water white,
   folded over their lives
   like wings of ducks
   settling on blood.

Ice from the Living Room

We're warped out of shape,
jaws tight
like antlers in the snow.
The cat pacing the house at night
daintily steps over what we were.
While your nostrils flare
into the wind sniffing spring thaw,
your hands lock on my hips
claiming the woman you say I am.

Only I
smell the tired rose petals
stuck to a stamp, the stale smell
of old letters and the last sweaty sheets
collected and dried into straw.
In the distance, between us,
tundra cracks into crystals
cold and firm as my profile.

You said:
I must dance or go mad
in this cocoon; frown when I ask
for your notes, thinking you quoted
some poet. I toss away your anger
with lines pulled from a Kleenex box.
The core of what we are hangs
trapped in cones of ice,
stalagma filling the living room.

The sky melts,
your ears turn north;
a jazz horn trapped in a bar
blows your hair.
Your hat tilts to hide your eyes
as you leave for the mating season
and I hold my wicked ways
in place.

The Mirror

How well she sits,
that lady
in the queenly caned-back chair.
My ex-husband's ex-wife
staring into the bright
surface where suburbs
are not reflected.
She scorns cotillions
black or white.
Sits, instead, dressed down,
daintily pouring beer,
inspecting the split ends
of her hair.
She is separated
from the world,
delicately filtered in shadows
squares and triangles
dancing through the chair.
The mocha light
paints fantastic things—
postage stamps, photos
coffee cups, copper babies—
like the pennies
she piles against the glass
of beer,
arranged and rearranged—
first a circle,
then a line like yellow cabs.
With those and a jack hammer
she could build a city,
make that glass surface
come alive.
Now, it's flat
without lines or freeways.

No crumbling brownstones
break the glaze,
no bombs or politics
scratch the children.
She offers a toast,
this lady,
a perfect hostess
to a perfect union.

Another Morning

I rise like an aging lizard
back gone bad
eyes glued with yesterday's sins
the alarm screams
its scorpion tail stings the mask
I call face
the light is ancient, my bones
too old to find
another morning awaiting me
no smile or kiss
just fuck-it and hurry into coffee
hurry life in
drumming strokes of time, knowing
2000 years from now
Anthro students will dig
their spades into my cheeks.

There Was An Old Woman...

Who sat in the gloom
Her empty pruned cheeks
Slowly worked on a piece of apple.
Last week they took the last tooth,
A broken brown bit of enamel,
And the juice ran sweet
Across her swollen gums.
There are spaces
Under the dusty brown skin
Of her thighs. Empty pockets
Where the last few globs of fat
Cling to her brittle bones.
Her knobby fingers move the blobs
In rhythm with her jaws,
As a gauzy dream of faces
Sweeps across her black brow.
She sits, unhurried,
Behind the steamy window
Of someone else's room.
She shoves her toes
Through another ghetto winter;
And when she meets a man,
She remembers——Harry?
Or was it Bill? She
Never looks them in the eyes
Anymore.

Educating the Coed

He gave her a piece
Of his mind,
Planted the foetus deep
In the zoo of hippocampus and sulcus.
The eunuch grew
In a shell of grey above the skull.
Its gnomed head pulsing,
Elbows smarting against the folds
And fissures; a mass of bloody pulp
In viscous float.

They came in calm awakening, those two.
Nostrils contracting, sucking air
That later crosses viaducts of red hue.
He reads her books to oil the works,
Synapses and switches, then shoots his wad
Across corpus and corpora, body and blood.
Noiseless ohms, twelve billion units,
More circuitry than AT&T
Found host before Education was born.

Her tongue is flecked with lead
From penciled notes, eyes ringed grey.
She swallows Eddie bit by bit,
A foetal speck wrapped in the spit
Of every word of her lecture notes;
Licking a bit of placenta from her chin,
Eddie breathes out and in, stronger
With each new thought.
Resting now on her landscaped lungs
Like a moon-man, in chambers semiluna.

Their love is logic, deductive;
An expertise of theories
Classified or rumored.
Her love comes slick like trading stamps,
Graded into her Romanesque apartments.
She waits for his subject to take root,
A strong staff, branching
Toward a hundred million cells
In sets of six, beating rhythm
Like fifteen men on a deadman.
And she lays like a ghostly monastery,
A naked sponge, clocking the tides
Of carbon and life.

Old Eddie hangs like a fossil
Beneath Adam's cage;
Advanced study for a B.A.,
A mammoth on museum display.
Twisting and curling, Ed filters the day.
Now she walks like a prof,
Her belly full of books.

For the Cheerleaders
of Garfield High

In pom-poms and perfume
They're picture perfect
Palm wine drinkers scream
As they spin and leap
Each motion set
For stop action
A flash of blackberry thigh
An arched neck
Lifting a satin chin
Then bursts of light
As they collapse
Giggling in rhyme
They take you back
To any hometown game
Backs like graceful strings
On a harp blend
And flow with their arms
Making music in space
Catching strains of the Sahara
They weave a cat's cradle
Of dreams, these girls
Who could wash rice
On a mud floor
Wearing mink.

The Dance

Red bulbs click on,
blue lights flash against the wall
where shadows move
elongated.
The thunk-thunk of a bass fiddle
is married to the message
of a drum.
Feet flash in rhythm.

In a dozen windows waffled against
the night sky, dancers sway
in a red and blue Picasso print.

They come from Toro
Mali and Chad
by way of Memphis
and the Great Northern.
My mind breaks clean
as the rhythm strips my bones
and splits them wide.
The ball of my foot joins the floor.
Flash——slam,
my heel lifts just in time.
One second later——swing,
hips snap quietly
and my toes join 40 others
sliding home.

The windows record each sway
in off-time.

In a window,
we dance a thousand lives;
on the floor,
time has a calling card
and that smell of death, I know,
is mine.

Arms snake skyward and down
mixing lights——red,
and red and blue.
Step——slide,
heads nod, hips suggest;
we chant the end.

And turn to the window
to see only
the night.

It's Familiar

My features have blended so
Well since years ago
When folks would
Look from my spindly legs
To my wide, spread mouth
And nose—nod their heads
Knowingly, age-wise crones
Keening through their gums
She'll do——in a pinch . . . yeah!

Still trapped in this civilized room
A world with a civilized door
My breath gulps up
Through nicotine, my smile thin
The walls rush in——noise
Exploding in bursts of color
Faces twisted, inane events
Repeated, the divided world
Chanting——we're together . . . yeah!

My lungs burst with sound
With echoed smoking yeah's
The groups are cut
Split and spread
Like peanut butter
On day-old bread
War builds the rhythm
A stale song for the poor
Mothers do it with words
While their sons break windows.

Fat white men with black cigars
Sisters hissing under puffy 'fros
Dap black pontificators in white cars
Roaring——together! together!
This music is freedom . . . yeah!
The beat is slow, small steps
Tiptoeing like a whore
Outside this door
I watch and wonder how
Long the sound will travel
Through time
The grinding teeth
The fists, the spit
Infinitely together, yeah!

Night People

young sweet thing
moving across the floor
everything exposed except
mother's milk
nods her head to the drummer's
delicate hands
his wasp waist bends, made supple
by needle point
fairy queen
caresses the floor
in front of him
as sweet thing shows her charms
and the queen in her arms
hides his chest hair and sly wink
under fluid rhythms
of the latest dance
the night people are out
rocking back on their heels
'chines parked out front
gleaming like their teeth
high gloss hogs
motors praying
ride as you pay
four gears, power drive
and posh comfort
blonde pigs for status
the night people are here
alive under a night sky
and soft ceiling light
male, black, and smooth
pushing muscle and skill
against the heat
of a pounding floor
moving flesh under night's dress
suggesting a better life

through soul ballet
as he stars
in his self made court
high——styling and hoping
some young thing will
buy the night life
and hump to keep
his body shining

News Report

it's going to rain again
the poets will scream of riots
and the writers will research
mothers as if their black bellies
carried the billowy black clouds of storms
their fingers keeping tune for dull grey thunder

Mama, can we measure you on a Richter scale
are you unaware that the warmth of your arms
becomes hot winds, still and quiet before the rain
the tears you cried when your child
lay crumpled on the ground after the first tree climb
washes anger from the crowded streets
or the slap of your hand against skin
for some childish trick finally stings
the roof of a prowl car with slick hail stones

is a satellite forecast
as bad as bringing home a note from school
and finally when it rains
will the poets quiet the world
with sweet words, as sweet smelling as wet spring

the tall thin sister swaying down the street
is unaware that she is a prairie wind
coiled tight, funneled into a high whine
tossing wheat and corn into the red frightened
face of a Kansas farm

a short chocolate lady tries fitting her bosom
into the confines of a bra, wincing
as the snapping band smarts her hand
flesh leaps from the folds, pushing air forward
and over, in forty or more turns
in Florida the force topples trees scatters
oranges into the sea, forecasters graph
the winds called she

the truth of such great gusts is gospel
and sung in mellow cocoa voice in storefront
churches, the satin lips of the sisters puff songs
sweet and low like the first movements blowing
Jamaica's shore before the tide is whipped unaware
into half an ocean or more, the froth
on those waves like lace cuffs holding good books
back at the churchfront store

a sweet chick smoking a cigar
sits beside a pocked kitchen table
crossing her legs causing small gusts
noting quite seriously the pattern of coffee stains
on the floor, unaware that as a poet she must write
each line furiously before the wind shifts
toward another who takes a fancy to words

and now the verse before the sports report
a fuzzy map, out of focus dead center
jumbled highs and lows, degrees overview
curving arrows going not everywhere
swinging out to sea, lost
finding its way into a small town's
surprise like the young round girl
who carried roses to Maine in wicker
flower words to pollinate poems
until they are forgotten found
awaking some sleeping critic

Index of First Lines

.

Index of First Lines